D0177496

BUSY PLACES

Football Stadium

Carol Watson

W

FRANKLIN WATTS

NEW YORK • LONDON • SYDNEY

It's Friday at the football stadium and the day before a match. People are working hard to get ready for the big day.

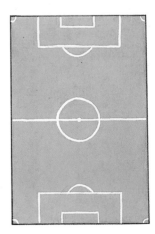

The Groundsman mows the pitch. He has to take special care of the grass so that the football teams can play well.

"That seems to be the right length," he says to himself. "Now it's time to paint on the lines clearly."

Other workers are doing
all kinds of repairs.
They fix the seats that are
loose, and mend and paint
anything that is damaged.
Then they check that all
the lights are working.

When they've finished outside,
the workmen check inside the stadium building.
"This light is broken, John," says one of them.
"We'll need to replace it."

It's match day! All through the morning
people come to the Box Office
to buy their tickets for the afternoon's game.
Ed has come to see his favourite team play.
"One ticket for today's match, please," he says.

Inside the stadium the Stewards have arrived.
It is their job to make sure the fans are looked after
and behave while the game is on.
The Supervisor tells them what to do.

Next the Stewards
search the stadium.
They look under
the seats to make
sure that everything
is safe.

Meanwhile, the
Security Guards
arrive. They will
ask anyone
who causes trouble
to leave.

While the Stewards get into position, Mr West, the Safety Officer, goes through his final check list.

"Everything is ready now," he says. "The fans can come in."

Inside the building the Kit Manager unlocks the Kit Room. This is where the team's football shirts and boots are kept. He puts the kit in the changing room ready for the players to put on.

At 1.30 p.m. the fans start to come in. One by one they walk through the turnstiles and go to their seats. The fans watch as the players "warm up" on the pitch.

Meanwhile, in the stadium kitchen the Chef is preparing lunch. "This will soon be ready to serve," he says.

Waiters take the food and drinks to the spectators who are in the private seating area.

In the control room the Police, Ambulance and Security staff have arrived for the match. They study the television screens, watching out for any problems inside or outside the stadium.

Up on a platform the
Television Cameraman
is ready. He hears
the crowds roar as the
two teams come out
onto the pitch.

It's 3.00 p.m. The Referee blows his whistle and the match begins. The stadium is full of fans waving and cheering for their teams.

"Come on, Trevor!" shouts one boy as he spots his favourite player kicking the ball.
"Queens Park Rangers!" chant the fans as they watch their team play.

At half-time the players have a rest. Ed goes to a kiosk to buy himself a hot drink.

The spectators in the private seating area have drinks together, too.

It's time for the second half to begin.
The fans are back in their seats
ready to watch the players in action again.

"Come on, Rangers!" chants the crowd as Trevor quickly "dribbles" the ball down the pitch.

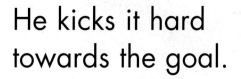

He kicks it hard towards the goal.

It's a goal! The crowd cheer as they think their team has scored. But no! The other team's goalkeeper has stopped the ball. The Rangers fans sit back in dismay.

The game is over.
The final whistle goes.
The supporters cheer
and wave as the players
run off the pitch.

The fans leave the stadium and head for home. When everyone has gone, it's time for the cleaners' work to begin.

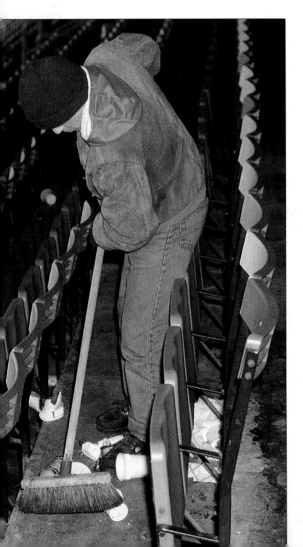